Family &
Money
Matters

*Life Lessons for
the New Generation*

Elaine King

First Edition

Kaabrah
PUBLISHING

Gold River, California

Family and Money Matters

WARNING – DISCLAIMER

Library of Congress Cataloging-in-Publication Data

King, Elaine, 1975-
Family & money matters: life lessons for the new generation/Elaine King. — 1st ed.
  p. cm.

  LCCN 2010936215
  ISBN-13: 978-0-9818322-1-0
  ISBN-10: 0-9818322-1-0

  1. Young adults—Finance, Personal. 2. Finance, Personal.
  3. Families—Economic aspects.
  I. Title. II. Title: Family and money matters

HG179.K56 2010   332.024'008'42   QBI10-600181

Printed in the United States of America.

Second Printing: November 2010

To my family, friends, and mentors
for giving me the ingredients
to write this book and
for sharing your life lessons with me.

Why You Need to Read this Book

Recently, I spoke to a theater full of high school students about the importance of getting a good education and having good financial habits. About five minutes into my presentation, I noticed many students looked confused or bewildered. It was as if I were speaking in a foreign language. And to most, I was.

Many of these kids will be the first generation in their families to graduate from college.

> Only 1 percent of 12th graders understand the basics of personal finance

One student was interested enough to ask, "How do I get paid to go to college?" At first, I didn't understand what he was asking me. I then realized he wanted to know about financial resources that might be available such as loans, grants, and scholarships. And, as I quickly learned, many of the other students in that theater did not know about any of this, either.

Most, also, didn't know a lot about saving, managing, and investing money. This is one of the main reasons why I wrote this book, and why you should read it. You must make sure that you—a member of our next generation—are empowered with basic knowledge and awareness of good financial habits so that you can begin building your personal well-being. None of us is born financially competent; we must learn it. I want this to be the start for you.

You also need to know that family dynamics are incredibly important in how you manage your money. The way you earn, save, invest, and protect your money is all about knowing yourself. And, to be able to know yourself better, you need to understand your family's values around money as well as its history and behavior.

Exploring your own family system is the key to discovering where your personal drive and attitudes about money originate. Throughout this book, I will explain why and how your family affects how you deal with money.

Enjoy!

~ *Elaine King*

Contents

Acknowledgements

I would like to thank a number of people without whom this book would never have been written. They encouraged or inspired me, and I will forever be grateful to them.

- ➡ My precious family, including my mom, dad, husband, grandparents, aunts, uncles, and cousins.

- ➡ My wonderful colleagues throughout my professional career.

- ➡ My dear clients and friends.

- ➡ My amazing editor, Anne Marie Smith, who added a rainbow of colors to my words and thoughts and shared her own personal stories.

I also want to thank the special people who took time out of their busy lives to review my manuscript:

- ➡ Charles W. Collier, Senior Philanthropic Advisor, Harvard University (www.tpi.org).

- Douglas K. Freeman, Senior Managing Director, First Foundation Advisors (www.ff-inc.com).

- Scott Galvin, Vice President of Education, Junior Achievement, Miami (www.jamiami.org).

- Barry Gottlieb, Founder and President, Coaching the Winners Edge (www.coachingthewinnersedge.com).

- Lee Hausner, Senior Managing Director, First Foundation Advisors (www.ff-inc.com).

- Kathy Wiseman, CEO, Working Systems (www.kathywiseman.com).

Thank you all so much.

1

What Makes You Tick?

W/here do you get your drive? What causes your mind, body, and soul to take action? According to British naturalist Charles Darwin (1809-1882), knowing what moves you and what triggers your actions are keys to your evolution.

Have you ever wondered why some days you are more energetic than on others? Well, there's a little engine inside of you—called your drive—that turns on and off. Your drive actually developed while you were still in your mother's womb.

So, why am I talking about drive when this is a book about money? Because your drive dictates whether you'll go to college, what kind of job or profession you'll have, how well you'll do at work, how much money you'll make over your lifetime, and how you'll handle your money.

Your drive is your internal locomotive that powers you forward to success and helps you achieve your dreams.

To understand the origin of your drive, you must take a closer look at your family and begin to explore its history. You need to find out what moves and motivates them. Why? Because as the old saying goes, the apple does not fall far from the tree. In other words,

instinctively, you may follow your family's example and not even realize it.

Recently, I had lunch with a very successful man. When I asked him where he got his "mojo," he answered, "My family. I don't know when it started exactly, but it was at least four generations ago that we, as a family, felt that we needed to be productive. You don't see many people in my family sitting still for a long period of time."

Here are responses I received from several young adults when I asked them the question, "What drives and motivates you?"

Susan, 18

Susan told me that her motivation comes from her parents. "They worked incredibly hard every day, but also found time to give us attention. My dad was well educated, bright, disciplined, and self-made. My mom focused on family relationships. Caring and compassion were her greatest gifts to me. Equally important were my elder sisters, who set the bar high."

Leo, 22

Leo told me that his drive comes from the positive reinforcement he received all of his life. "I was a great student and always at the top of my class. My parents were supportive and told my siblings and me that anything that we wanted to do was possible. I never heard 'It can't be done.' I heard, 'Try it.'"

Darnell, 25

"My drive came from watching my father work hard and achieve success at an early age," says Darnell. "He died when we were teenagers, though, and we struggled to survive without him. This, however, led me to want to be the best at what I do."

Maria, 28

Maria says that succeeding together as a family motivates her. What gets her up in the morning? "My kids, and doing everything I can to contribute to their health and well-being. Family values are one of the most important elements that define what and who we become in our adult lives."

Anya, 20

Anya says, "I'm motivated by my ability to be independent and at peace with all of the beautiful things that Mother Nature gives us. My father taught me to listen to the birds, appreciate the colors of the sky, and meditate."

Peter, 19

"I'm motivated by a sense of accomplishment. My parents instilled this in me since I was a child. Making a difference in someone's life also motivates me," Peter says.

Joachim, 22

Joachim is motivated by having ownership of a project or task, and by leaving something better than it was before he gets involved. "There's also a selfish aspect to what motivates me. I want to do my best, be better than my competition, and stand out."

You and Your Drive

I'd like you to take a moment and think about you and your drive. Grab a pen or pencil and answer the following questions to the best of your ability.

➡ What motivates you?

➡ What makes you happy and turns on your engine?

➡ What is your passion in life?

➡ What are your top three life goals (your mission)?

➡ If money were not an issue, what would you do this year to accomplish your goals?

➡ What are your biggest obstacles, besides money, in achieving your goals?

➡ Who in your family do you think influenced your drive the most, and why?

2
Families & Financial Literacy

Although financial skills are learned, you either inherited your values and attitudes about money as a part of your family's legacy, or they are innate and instinctual—or some of both.

Some think that their families have nothing to do with the way they manage their money, but I believe that family has a lot to do with the way the next generation thinks about and behaves with money. You may not necessarily manage money identically, but the values and attitudes your parents and grandparents had towards money contributed greatly to the relationship you have with it today.

A client of mine, Paul, is a very successful businessperson. His father was also very successful at one time, but then lost it all and was forced to leave his children. Paul grew up with an enormous drive to be the best, to be involved, and to help the community. He has founded and built two companies from scratch.

What Is Your Family's Financial Literacy?

In my experience working with families, financial literacy often influences a family's value system, its attitudes, and its emotional behavior. I have worked with families who sacrifice a great amount to provide the largest possible inheritance for their children. I also work with others who want to spend every last cent before they die.

> Financial literacy is the ability to make knowledgeable and successful decisions about using and managing your money.

To discover *your* family's financial literacy, you must first understand the dynamics of each of your family members.

For example, I always wondered why my father asked my mother, "Do you need it or do you want it?" before she bought something of higher value. Interestingly, I learned that my grandfather also used to ask my grandmother the same question.

Financial literacy is a generational chip that you are born with, and unless you learn about your own background you will not understand your tendencies and behavior. In your lifetime, this treasure from the past, plus your own ingredients, will help you build your financial personality and drive.

It was not until I started learning more about families, and how they work, that I began to understand how my family and its history influenced my financial behavior.

I'm originally from Peru. My family began teaching me the value of money from the moment I could walk. At a very young age, they sent me to buy ice cream on my own so I would begin to learn how to negotiate—a behavior not common culturally in the United States. They also taught me the importance of hard work and the value of money.

I have a close friend who cringes at the thought of doing his taxes and organizing his bills. I suspect the reason is that his parents dreaded and avoided managing their money like the plague.

What Is Success?

For some families, success is a specific number. Actually, success is about more than money. In his book, *Outliers*, author Malcolm Gladwell interviews many famous and wealthy people about success. Their answers were not all about money. They said that success had more do to with reaching their own highest capacities, working hard, and making the best of what they made.

Wealth is nothing without passion. Working towards your passion will give you unlimited returns.

Emotions & Money

Growing up in Peru, I learned about both the value and the emotional component of money due to an unstable economic and political environment. At that time, inflation was high and terrorism was rampant. We never knew if or when we'd be without water or electricity.

Because of my upbringing, today I look at my finances as part of a bigger picture. I look at my income and savings and carefully decide how to invest, manage, and share my money. I rarely spend money based on my emotions or impulses.

Most families, however, invest little time planning for their futures. This causes anxiety to accumulate and emotions to overpower reasoning. Saving for retirement or buying an insurance policy to protect the family is usually very low on the priority scale because it involves giving up things that they value now—a car, a vacation, a bigger home.

In theory, most people are very committed to long-term goals yet, in the moment, temptations appear before us and our plans fly out the door. Reason and emotion often compete inside our brains.

Over the past 15 years, I have worked as a wealth planner with many, many families—some of whom came to the U.S. with limited means and some of whom inherited their wealth. From my experience, immigrant parents often struggle with emotions and money. They want and tend to give their children everything they did not have.

Families' lives are also affected by patterns and circumstances that force them to act with a "sink or swim" mentality. Examples include:

➡ Divorces or second marriages.

➡ Job loss.

➡ Arrests and prosecutions.

➡ Adoption or blended families.

Delayed Gratification

Delayed gratification is the ability to wait in order to get something that you want. Human beings did not experience delayed gratification during the early stages of our evolution, so it goes against our nature. We hunted when we were hungry and we ate what we killed, right then and there. Immediate gratification is a primal instinct.

This could very well explain part of what's happening in today's world—the immediate gratification of lenders, and of buyers' impulses to nab "hot properties" at higher prices than their market value.

> Delayed gratification is also called impulse control, will power, and self-control.

Because of our propensity to buy what we want when we want it, it's often very difficult to inspire people to save for the future.

Fortunately, my family taught me the difference between need and want at a young age. "Waiting and patience will pay off at the end," they always said. Every Saturday morning, my parents would give me an allowance and remind me to save half of it for a rainy day.

Studies have shown that if you begin to practice delayed gratification—for example waiting to play a video game until you've finished studying for a test—and make it a habit, you will increase your chances of achieving your life goals.

Family & Your Financial Behavior

At a workshop I conducted recently for young professionals, I asked them, "What role did your family play in your financial behavior?" Here are some of the responses I received.

Kendra, 26

"My family has had a major influence in my success and finances. They've been great role models—working hard, sacrificing, and being dedicated and supportive. They taught me to pursue my passion."

Manuela, 25

"My parents taught me to be content with what I have, not with what I want. I appreciate the simple things in life, such as a rose over a bouquet. My parents taught me that honesty should win out over money every time. No exceptions."

Greg, 29

"My financial behavior was greatly influenced by my parents. My father was a reluctant spender. He and my mom have been, and still are, big savers. But while they are thrifty, they are not cheap. Until I was in college, they rarely used a checkbook and never owned a credit card. They always used cash for everything. If they did not have the cash, they did not buy it. But somehow, they managed to provide us with everything we needed."

Briona, 21

"My dad had no cash other than coins in the house. One time, he gave my sister a big jar of coins and told her to take it to the bank to get bills to buy a dress. I was mortified. I remember thinking, 'All we have is coins?' Around the same time, my father threw a company picnic for his workers, some of whom knocked on our front door regularly asking for 'loans' that I'm certain were never paid back. I looked around the picnic grounds and thought, 'All these people depend on my father.' I vowed never to ask him for money again—and I didn't. I got my first part-time job at age 15, worked through college, and graduated a year early to save money on tuition."

Dileep, 24

"My parents taught me to learn to love business and finance. From my father, I learned budgeting and tracking every cent. I didn't receive my allowance until the checkbook was balanced and I reported where every nickel had gone. From my mother, I learned how to negotiate and purchase."

Lola, 25

"My parents were always open to talking about money issues. It was never a taboo subject like it is in several of my friends' families. Although financially successful, they were conservative in how they displayed their wealth."

The Meaning of Money

Money often creates dependent attitudes, values, and behaviors in children. These children then grow up to be dependent young adults who don't understand the meaning of money and think it's a right, not something you must work hard for.

One day, I was in the grocery store standing in line behind a woman and her young son. The boy, about seven years old, was standing at the candy rack and asked his mom if he could have a candy bar. She said, "No, I don't have enough money." He started fussing and complaining. He said, "Why can't you just go to the wall at the bank? They've got plenty of money." That mom, hopefully, sat down with her son later and explained how the money gets into the wall.

> The word "money" originates from the Roman fertility goddess Moneta, in whose temple the first money was minted.

My friend's nephew, Nick, is 14 years old. He loves money but doesn't like to work for it. He wants to play video games or watch TV all of the time. He certainly doesn't want to do his homework or chores, let alone clean his room. One day my friend asked, "Nick, if you don't do your homework, how are you going to get into a college? And, if you don't get into a college, what kind of job are you going to get? How will you make money to support yourself?" Nick mumbled, "I want to play games for a living." My friend threw up her arms and said, "Well, that will buy you a tent and a can of beans under a bridge. Good luck!"

What Does Money Mean to You?
I have some more questions for you. Grab your pen or pencil again.

➡ What does money mean to you?

➡ What would you do for a day without money?

➡ What did your parents teach you about handling money?

➡ What have your parents taught you about delayed gratification? How do they encourage you to wait and make it worthwhile?

➡ How does your family handle delayed gratification?

3

You Are
What You
Are Taught

One day, I had an appointment with a man who brought all of his financial information in with him. As I began to look it over, he said to me, "I'm 70 years old and I want to know if I can retire now. I've been working nonstop since I was 18. I planned on retiring at 68, but my daughter lost her job two years ago and she can't support herself."

I asked him how much he's helping her out. "Well, I built her a house next to mine so she doesn't have to pay rent and to give her some independence, and I pay all of her bills." When I asked how old his daughter was, he told me, "She's 37."

How could he possibly think he could retire? He's given his daughter no incentive to get back on her feet, so he'll be supporting her until he becomes ill or dies. I feel sorry for him, and I feel sorry for his daughter.

> Fifty-three percent of parents agree that their children think money grows on trees.

Another client came to my office worried that she will not be able to survive. I asked her what her net worth was and she told me $10 million. That seems like plenty, right? But when I asked her what her expenses were, she said, "Well, I pay my daughter's mortgage, my grandchildren's college tuitions, my other son's business loan..." And on and on. Her expenses added up to $1 million a year. She is 65 years old. At that rate, she will run out of money in ten years. I told her she needed to have a talk with her family. Like the previous man, this mother taught her children very little about money. They feel entitled because the parents allow them to be.

Jeffrey, a self-made millionaire, said his parents struggled to make a comfortable living, so he learned from an early age to work and save. He's a very busy and successful man whose only worry is that his children will grow up not understanding the value of money since he has accumulated more than they'll every need. "But," said Jeffrey, "if I leave them too much, it might rob them of the joy of success and achievement."

Laura and Don spent every cent of their retirement money helping their children and grandchildren. They now have only their Social Security income to live on. They just filed for bankruptcy and will lose their home. "We have no one to blame but ourselves," says Laura. "Here's what we learned: Help your kids, but don't make it so easy that they can't help themselves."

Warren Buffett, one of the world's richest men, plans to pass the bulk of his fortune on to the Bill and Melinda Gates Foundation, leaving only a portion to his children. Says Buffett, "A very rich person should leave his kids enough to do anything, but not enough to do nothing."

Eugene Lang, best known for creating the "I Have A Dream" Foundation, shares Mr. Buffett's thoughts about the matter. So far, he has given away more than half of his fortune. He paid for his three children's education, but has always expected them to become self-sufficient.

Forbes magazine's editor-in-chief Steve Forbes says, "How kids handle their circumstances depends on how they were brought up." So, if you learn to respect and manage money early in life, and if you learn that a successful life is a productive life, you are more likely to live those lessons.

The great news is that anyone can learn—including you. You don't have to be 100 percent of what you learned in your youth. You can educate yourself and adapt your ways any time you choose.

Jared's Story
Julie and Justin married in their early 20's while still in school. They both worked full time to pay for their

educations. They had to sell their car and musical instruments to be able to keep studying. They learned to appreciate the value of a dollar.

After they graduated and got jobs, they had a baby whom they named Jared. They decided early on that they would teach Jared the value of a dollar, too. They felt it was the greatest gift they could give him.

At five, he was given an allowance along with options— he could either spend all of it at once or save a portion and buy something bigger later. His parents discussed the pros and cons of doing each with him. At seven, Jared started to do more chores than he was assigned so he would earn a bigger allowance.

If he needed more money, for whatever reason, he had to fill out a request form to explain why and what he needed the money for. Requests were sometimes not granted if his reasons weren't sound.

Jared was challenged to get good grades in school and was rewarded when he did. By 11, he had saved enough to invest in the stock market—money he planned to use to pay for his college education.

He graduated from college and decided to go to graduate school. His dad paid for half of the cost and Jared paid for the other half. Jared completed the 24-month program in ten months and found a great job right away. He bought a small condominium soon after. His dad offered to pay half, but Jared said, "No, Dad, thank you, but you've done enough." Clearly, Jared had learned what he was taught.

The message? Jared discovered that saving was a very important component in gaining independence and freedom.

About My Family

The King-Chiong and Fuentes-Cole families immigrated to Peru in 1895 from England, Spain, and China. In the process, they fought battles, lost loved ones, started businesses, and lost fortunes. Their experiences are a treasure chest of lessons for me. Three characteristics they all had included:

➡ Hard workers.

➡ Valued education.

➡ Believed in continual self-improvement.

Let me tell you a bit about them.

My dad's family

My father's parents were both born in 1917. My grandfather was an only child from a second marriage. His father was very strict and was often hard on him. This contributed to my grandfather's philosophy about discipline.

My grandmother, of Chinese descent, was the second of six children. Her father had several businesses in Hong Kong. Since transportation was by boat, it took months to go back and forth so my grandmother attended school in Hong Kong.

Her father died from bubonic plague, leaving her mother a widow with six young children. Not knowing what to do, she lost most of her inheritance in bad investments. This taught my grandmother the effects of money on families. It also taught her to be a tough negotiator.

My grandparents met in school when they were 14 years old. They both graduated with honors in Chemical Engineering. After much family dispute, they were married in 1945. Their dream was to use their educations to help their community, so they decided to open a pharmacy.

My grandparents bought a house across the street from their pharmacy and had four children. By this time, they owned several pharmacies and worked a lot, but always had lunch with their children and helped them with their homework.

All of their children and grandchildren worked in the family business at some point. All of them studied and became successful professionals.

My dad

My dad was taught early in life that he must be a productive member of the world. His parents also told him that if he worked smart and hard, success would follow. He saw how hard his parents worked and he developed his values from them.

He studied industrial engineering at a very tough university, paying most of his way. Upon graduating, he was offered a scholarship to study for his MBA (Masters of Business Administration). Armed with his degrees, he was recruited for a position at a Fortune 500 company. He climbed quickly through the ranks, becoming Head of Sales in Latin America. Due to his position, our family had to move to a different country every couple of years. New culture, new house, new friends—it was difficult but it helped all of us become more adaptable.

He now has his own consulting firm that works with Fortune 100 companies. He still works until 11:00 p.m. many days, and talks happily about the massive workload he always has. He's a workaholic, but because he's passionate about what he does he loves every minute of it. I have inherited this trait from him.

My dad is extremely careful with and practical about money, but he also aligns his spending to his values. He spends money freely on vacations and family gatherings, but he is very careful about spending on material things and justifies every expense.

My mother's family

My great-grandfather, who was British, was killed at age 30 by politicians who thought he knew too much. My great-grandmother was pregnant with her third child when her husband died. As a young widow, she had to work very hard to support her children.

My grandfather's family was from the Iberian Peninsula in Spain. His family immigrated to Peru for religious reasons.

My mother's parents met while they both worked for the Peruvian government in 1951. They were 11 years apart in age. My grandfather was an adventurer who jumped out of planes and was on the government's equestrian team, all while studying to be an attorney. He was also the type of person who would give all when someone was in need. I remember his doorbell ringing constantly for "favors," including consultations, representation in court, and advice.

My grandmother is a hard worker, very driven, and extremely creative. She became a fashion designer, making clothes for boutiques, travelling all over the world, and always being up to date with the latest trends. She's now a well-respected artist.

She and my grandfather had two children, a girl and a boy, who both grew up to become successful educators in languages, business, science, and math. They also are devoted to helping their communities and the next generation.

My mom

My mom studied to be a teacher. She started working at the age of 18 in a pre-school. Once she received her degree, she taught at elementary, high school, and university levels. She now teaches Spanish to executives of Fortune 500 companies.

She was brought up to be a wife and mother, so her parents did not fully encourage her when they found out she had applied for a job. That did not stop her. She is a problem solver and needs to be busy constantly. She is not a 9 to 5 office worker, though. Instead, she is more of a free spirit who values peace of mind and work quality over quantity.

My mom is extremely generous with everything she has, including her time. She has always encouraged every dream I've ever had. She is not attached to material things. She believes in spiritual growth and the evolution of the soul and the power of self healing. She always tells me that everything happens for a reason and that there are many lessons to learn from each experience. I have inherited this from her.

My family lessons

Here are the lessons I have learned from my family:

➡ **Have a plan.** My parents taught me to evaluate before acting and always to ask myself, "Where does this fit into the plan?"

➡ **Live below your means**. My dad told me to allocate a set percentage of savings before spending.

➡ **Never stop learning**. "No one can take away your education," my mom used to say.

➡ **Follow your passion.** I learned to strive to do something better each day.

➡ **Relationships are important to your well-being.** My grandfather told me we are responsible for the quality of our relationships.

➡ **Get involved.** My parents told me that it was very important to share what you know with others.

Other People's Family Lessons

I have talked with hundreds of people, asking them to share lessons they learned about money from family members. Here are just a few.

Rhonda

"My mother always told us to save for a rainy day. She also encouraged me to enjoy life, but to be careful when choosing things on impulse. She encouraged me to have a 'fun fund' to buy my favorite things without guilt."

Caesar

"Some lessons I learned from my mother include, save bread for the winter, don't spend more than what you have, don't ask for or lend money because it can ruin relationships, and it's better to have one bird in hand than 100 flying."

Tinesha

"A lesson my parents taught me is, realize our blessings are not material things but are things such as our health and relationships."

Eric

"My dad taught me that money is a commodity to exchange goods for something I want. Beyond security, money means accomplishment—a bridge to my goals. It does not mean all in life to me."

Jackie

"My grandfather taught me to make sure my work is meaningful and beneficial to the community. My grandmother taught me that a penny saved is a penny earned. My dad taught me to put my money to work for me."

Julio

"My dad always told me that education is the engine that will propel me to opportunity, and to follow my passion and the money will follow. He also told me to never appreciate anything as much as that which I've earned with my own hard work and sweat."

Marco

"Various family members taught me a lot including, you should only buy what you can afford, avoid long term debt unless it's for a home or business, be aware of your investments, buy with cash, and be happy with what you can afford."

Tina

"My dad taught me to always have a contingency plan."

You & Your Family Lessons

It's your turn again. Answer the following questions.

➡ What family lessons do you believe have made a real difference in who you are today?

➡ What are some things that can be improved upon in your family of origin?

➡ What are you doing (or going to do) to balance your family's financial behavior and your attitudes about money?

4

On Debt
& Budgeting

L iving beyond our financial capacity results in
overspending and debt. We all know that we
should live with less than what we have, but we
often let our emotions overrule our brains and we
reward ourselves with things we can't afford. Many
times, we justify our overspending by telling ourselves,
"I work hard. I deserve it."

For others, circumstances beyond their control plunge
them into debt—they had to help a family member,
someone became ill and didn't have health insurance, or
the breadwinner of the family lost a job.

Regardless of the reasons, 70 percent of families in
America live paycheck to paycheck with the majority of
their income going to pay down their debt (or not).
Many people struggle with their debt for two years

before turning to bankruptcy. Personal bankruptcy filings in the United States increased nearly 350 percent between 1980 and 2005.

> **Bankruptcy is** a legal declaration that you are unable to pay your debts.

Sally

Sally is the breadwinner in her family. She works very hard every day to make her family proud. She's a doctor and makes a high six-figure salary. She's also a very successful community leader. One day, she received a call from a creditor. To her surprise, she had managed to get them deep into **debt**, which is an amount owed to a person or an organization for money borrowed.

Christine

Christine is a happily married professional with three children. Her husband put them into debt by falling for several business scams. Christine is now worried that they won't have money for their children's education, and they've set aside nothing for their retirement.

William

William won $16 million in a lottery. Within a year, not only did he spend the entire $16 million, but he also racked up an additional $1 million in debt. He now lives off of his $450-a-month Social Security checks.

Why do you think this happened to these people?

Budget? What's a Budget?

A personal **budget**, the first step in building a financial plan, distributes future personal income towards expenses, savings, and debt repayment. It's astounding how many people do not have budgets or, if they do, their budgets are often not realistic, or they do not live within them.

For many people, "budget" is a dirty word. Why do you think that is? Many think that because you live with a budget, you don't have enough money. On the contrary, if you live within a budget, you will have enough.

For example, if you are disciplined and you account for all of your spending, then you can allocate savings to specific things such as a travel, music, or going out to eat.

One young person I spoke with recently told me that his parents thought that living within a budget was not "proper," and never encouraged him to follow one. Now, he's constantly struggling with holding himself accountable for his expenses.

The number of 18 to 24 year olds declaring bankruptcy has increased 96 percent in the past 10 years.

Another said, "When I was young, my parents always gave me what I needed without hesitation, so I never learned about budgeting. Now, I'm in debt up to my ears."

How can we learn to budget or to teach others to budget if we have not been taught how to do it?

5

Managing
Your Money

Finches are small songbirds with colorful plumage. Approximately 14 different species of finches live on the Galapagos Islands. One year, an El Niño season weather pattern resulted in an oversupply of food. This excess food supply drastically affected the finch population. Their structure was disrupted, most grew bigger than expected, and the population expanded enormously. Shortly thereafter, the food supply went back to normal. Many of the birds that lacked the capacity to self regulate their

food consumption died. Those that—despite the abundance—managed their food intake, survived.

I liken this finch situation to how some Americans live beyond their means. Since 1980, Americans have consumed more than they have produced, and have lived far beyond their available financial resources.

Meet the Johnsons

The Johnsons were once a successful family consisting of Nora and Phillip and their two daughters. Nora and Phillip both had great careers that provided their family with an abundance of everything they needed and wanted. They didn't have a formal budget so most of the purchases they made were "as needed" versus planned.

They felt that stocks and bonds were risky due to an experience one of their grandparents had many years earlier. So, instead, they invested in real estate thinking that it was more secure. Their parents before them, after all, were able to make a living from buying and selling property.

When interest rates were low and money supply was high, Nora and Phillip bought multiple properties and overextended their credit during the rise of the market. Unfortunately, once the real estate market crashed they were no longer able to keep their properties. They are considering bankruptcy.

Meet the Garcias

The Garcias are business owners whose hard work has paid off. Ron and Sara Garcia have accumulated more wealth than they and their four children will ever need in their lifetimes.

Ron and his wife, however, raised their children with little structure or discipline. Now Ron feels that his children view him as their own personal ATM machine. His biggest worry is that they'll never learn the value of achievement and money.

About Money Management

Does our species have the capacity to self regulate? Yes, we absolutely do. But to do so, we must:

➡ Become financially competent.

➡ Proactively and consciously manage our money.

An **asset** is something valuable that you own, benefit from, or have use of. An asset could be a house you own, your education, or your personality. One of the most important assets you have—aside from your intellectual, social, and spiritual assets—is your financial asset; that is, your ability to earn money. The most successful individuals in the world are those who followed their passion, reaped a financial reward, and had the discipline to defend that reward at all costs.

In this chapter, you'll learn the principles of money management, including:

➡ Knowing your net worth.

➡ Setting up the appropriate bank accounts.

➡ Understanding debt.

➡ Understanding credit ratings.

➡ Managing credit cards.

Managing your money isn't hard, but it's a critical skill for you to learn so that you can set yourself and your family up for future security.

Knowing Your Net Worth

The first step in managing your money is to take inventory of what you have already by calculating your **net worth**, which are your assets minus your liabilities. Grab a piece of paper and I'll tell you how.

1. At the top of the page write the word "Assets." Underneath it, list all of your assets including money in your bank and investment accounts, money in your wallet, and the estimated current value of any personal property you own (house, car, jewelry, and so on). Add up your assets to get a total.

2. Write the word "Liabilities." A **liability** is a legal obligation to pay a debt. Under that heading, list all of your liabilities including credit card balances, student loans, auto loans, lines of credit, mortgages, business loans, and so on. Add up your liabilities to get a total.

> A good practice is to update your net worth at least once a year so you always know where you are.

3. Subtract your liabilities from your assets. This is

your current personal net worth. Understanding this will help you plan for the future.

Your Other Assets & Liabilities

When you calculate your net worth I also suggest you calculate the net worth of your intellectual, social, and spiritual assets and liabilities to help you understand what you have going for you and against you in achieving your goals.

What are your strengths in terms of education, human and community interaction, and self-growth?

What are your liabilities in these same areas? Do you lack a higher education? Do you have a tendency not to be social and build relationships? Do you not constantly seek to grow as a person?

Setting Up Your Bank Accounts

Money in your pocket or in a piggy bank is easily lost or stolen. Banks keep your money safe. Additionally, banks pay you interest on your money because they use it elsewhere until you need it. Open both a checking account and a savings account, and get a debit card at the same time.

Checking Accounts

Use your checking account to pay bills and daily expenses. Once you deposit money into your checking account you can then either write checks or use your debit card to pay your bills. Of course, only write checks if you have money in your account or your check will bounce and the bank will charge you a hefty fee.

Savings Accounts

Savings accounts provide you with a place to stash money for emergencies or planned purchases. You can allocate an automatic percentage of your earnings to this account before you pay your bills. While there, it accumulates and grows because banks also typically pay you interest on your savings account.

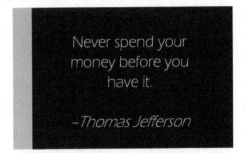

Never spend your money before you have it.

–*Thomas Jefferson*

Debit Cards

Debit cards—also called check cards and ATM cards—look like a credit card but function like a check. When you use one, money is automatically deducted from your checking account. Make sure you have a debit card with overdraft protection to avoid paying additional fees.

Reviewing Your Accounts

Develop the habit of monitoring your monthly statements for accuracy. Review every transaction including checks, online bill payments, withdrawals from the ATM, and charges on your debit card. Doing so ensures that you know how much is in each account so you don't spend money you don't have, and avoids the hassle of clearing up bounced checks.

Understanding Debt

Everyone should understand debt before getting too deep into it. There are two types of debt:

- → **Good debt** includes things that have the capacity to appreciate—produce more wealth—in the future (for example, your education, a house, or a business).

- → **Bad debt** includes items that tend to depreciate in the future (for example, clothing, electronics, cars, and boats).

Why is this distinction important? The difference could mean long-term financial success or drowning in a sea of bills.

Managing Credit Cards

Credit cards, on the other hand, allow you to buy now and pay later. Too much credit card debt is one of the main reasons people file for bankruptcy in the United States. However, there are times that credit cards must be used, such as when you are short on cash for large purchases, or to build credit when first starting out.

> **Warning: Credit card companies allow you to pay only a portion of your bill, but they will charge you high interest rates on the amount you don't pay back by the due date.**

Taking high interest rates into account, a $1,000 purchase on your credit card can end up costing you $3,400 and 22 years to pay back if you make only the minimum monthly payment. So you could, potentially, still be paying for a brand new wardrobe more than 15 years after you donated it to a charity! This is why I 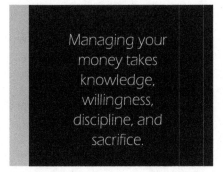 always recommend not to charge more than you can pay off within a month or two.

Which Card to Choose

When choosing which credit card to apply for, compare:

- Costs, including annual percentage rates, late fees, cash advance fees, and balance transfer fees.

- Features, including the grace period, credit limit, how widely the card is accepted, rewards, and customer service.

Guidelines for Credit Cards

Here are guidelines about credit cards I recommend that you follow:

- ➡ Have two credit cards at the most. Do not apply for every card offer you receive in the mail; this is the quickest road to racking up bad debt.

- ➡ Never spend more than 50 percent of your credit line.

- ➡ Always pay off the outstanding balance on time.

- ➡ Avoid charging things that you can pay for in cash. This way, you avoid additional fees.

- ➡ Never abuse your credit cards.

Understanding Credit Ratings

Now, let's talk about credit ratings. Credit is important because, like reputation, it's very easy to lose and takes many years to build back up. Establishing a strong credit rating is vital for your future financial transactions. Having strong credit saves you money in the end. You need strong credit to get a good interest rate when buying cars and houses, and when applying for car insurance. You also need a strong credit rating to rent an apartment or house.

> Having a bad credit history can cost you in high interest rates and in refusals of loans and credit cards.

When applying for a job your prospective employer may look at your credit scores, available on credit reports, as reference. A strong credit rating also determines whether you can obtain a college loan.

The keys to a strong credit rating include:

- ➡ Always pay your bills on time.

- ➡ Keep balances low on credit cards.

➡ Pay more than the minimum amount due.

Credit reports are managed by three companies: Equifax, Experian, and TransUnion. Once you begin establishing credit, you should run a credit report once a year to verify its accuracy. Report any incorrect information immediately to have it corrected.

You can run a free credit history report on yourself at www.annual creditreport.com.

Sixty-five percent of the report is about your payment history and how much you owe. It includes a full history of your bank accounts, loans, and other debt. If you file for bankruptcy, it will remain on your credit report for seven to ten years.

Insurance

The two most important insurance policies you should have while you are an independent, single person (if you have no dependents and do not own a home) are:

➡ Health insurance.

➡ Car insurance.

According to recent Census Bureau statistics, drivers under the age of 22 accounted for 29.4 percent of all car accidents, despite being only 13.4 percent of the driving population. Another study showed that teens and young adults admitted to the emergency room without health insurance were in debt for several years after college, and some were forced to drop out of school to work and pay off their bills.

Later in life, as you buy a home, have a family, and build a business, there are very important insurance policies you need to protect yourself and your family including life insurance, home insurance, and disability insurance to name a few.

6

Planning & Saving Your Money

Bears have the ability to plan ahead to survive. Approximately three months before winter they eat fatty foods that keep them full for months. Then, knowing they will not have enough food during the winter months, they discipline their bodies to eat smaller amounts than normal. Similar to squirrels, mice, and beavers, bears store food to eat later.

Like bears, we must learn how to preserve our resources to survive.

Meet the Wongs

The Wong family is highly educated and hard working. Adam Wong's salary is modest. Adam and his wife, Candace, have three college-age children. The Wongs plan for everything. They plan their vacations carefully, pay their credit cards each month on time and in full, have college savings funds for their children, and have planned for their retirement in five years.

Meet the Polsons

Rick Polson has a very successful global business. He's a highly trained individual who followed in his father's footsteps. Professionally, he has achieved a lot. On the home front, however, he has been absent during most of his marriage and he and wife, Amanda, are estranged. He's now in his 50's and suffering from health issues, which keep him from attending to his business. He has no savings nor does he have a contingency plan.

About Planning & Saving

Planning and saving your money involves:

➡ Creating a budget and a savings plan.

➡ Saving money.

➡ Justifying and tracking every purchase.

➡ Monitoring your progress.

As you can see, like managing your money, planning and saving your money is simple but you must be proactive and disciplined about it.

Creating a Budget & Savings Plan

Budgeting and planning are extremely critical in achieving financial independence. Most of you will work very hard for the money you earn. What's most important is not how much money you make but what you do with the money. A budget helps you establish priorities. A savings plan helps you make wise decisions about spending.

"Good plans shape good decisions. That's why good planning helps to make elusive dreams come true." This quote, by author Lester Bittel, is truly apt here. Studies, by the way, have shown that when you plan you are happier.

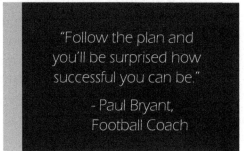

"Follow the plan and you'll be surprised how successful you can be."

- Paul Bryant,
Football Coach

So, before you do anything else you must create a budget, which you then use to create your savings plan.

Five Steps To Becoming Budget Wise

To create your budget, take out a clean sheet of paper.

1. At the top of the page write "Monthly Income." List all of your income sources. Add them up. Subtract the taxes you must pay on your income. Taxes include:

   - Federal (10 to 35 percent, depending on how much you earn).

   - Social Security (6.2 percent).

- Medicare (1.45 percent).
- State (varies by state, but ranges between 1 and 11 percent; check online for your state's tax rate).

2. Subtract the total taxes from your income and divide result by 12. This is the amount of money for which you must create a spending plan and budget.

3. Write "Fixed Expenses." **Fixed expenses** are the costs you have that stay approximately the same each month. You can pull these from the liabilities you listed when you were calculating your net worth. Add to those other fixed expenses you have, such as monthly rent, insurance payments, and utilities. Be sure to allocate 10 to 15 percent of your income to a savings category.

4. Next, write "Variable Expenses" on the page. **Variable expenses** are costs over which you have choices. They include items such as groceries, gasoline, clothing, travel, entertainment costs such as dining out, movies, music, concerts, and so on. Subtract your fixed and variable expenses from your monthly income.

How did you do? Did you come out ahead with money to spare or are you spending more than you have? It's pretty eye opening, isn't it?

Brandon, 23

I helped a young client of mine put his budget together recently. Brandon is two years out of college and makes $38,000 per year as a pharmaceutical sales representative.

I calculated his taxes and then asked him what all of his current fixed and variable costs were. After adding everything up, I showed him the very scary tally...

Brandon's Budget	
Monthly Income	
Salary	$38,000.00
Total taxes	$7,858.00
Annual net income	$30,142.00
Monthly (net/12)	**2,511.83**
Fixed Expenses	
Rent	$1,200.00
Student loan payment	$250.00
Car payment	$400.00
Utilities	$120.00
Credit card payment	$85.00
Insurance	$100.00
Total	**$2,155.00**
Variable Expenses	
Groceries	135.00
Gasoline	50.00
Dining out	150.00
Entertainment	200.00
Total	**535.00**
Grand total	**-178.17**

"You're about $180 short each month," I said.

Brandon shook his head and said, "No wonder I'm always broke."

"And," I told him, "if you keep this up, your credit card debt will increase because you are spending more than what you make, which you'll then find nearly impossible to pay down because, again, you don't have enough extra cash. It's an endless circle. I see it happen all the time."

I went on, "And Brandon, this doesn't include putting aside anything for an emergency fund or retirement."

"What should I do?" Brandon asked.

"First, you need to stop funding your excess spending with your credit cards. To do so, you need to cut other expenses. Look for a less expensive place to live. If you can't then you must reduce what you spend on dining out and entertainment."

"But that's my fun. You're asking me to not have fun?" Brandon said.

"I'm suggesting that you find less expensive fun. You're a smart guy. Get creative. Then, when you get a raise or promotion and your income increases, you can then adjust your budget to include some of those things again. You must think long term to get ahead."

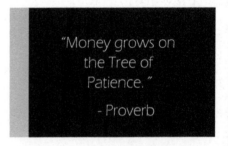

"Money grows on the Tree of Patience."

- Proverb

Saving is an act of delayed gratification. It's hard sometimes, but it's worth it in the end. The prize is much better. I promise you.

Is *your* debt growing at a higher rate than your savings account? If it is, you can do something about it now before you go down as captain of your sinking ship.

Three Steps to Plan Your Dreams

Once you have a budget, use it to create your savings plan. You want your plan to be specific, not vague. Good plans describe what, how, and by when.

To create your plan:

1. Identify your goals.

2. List the actions you need to take to achieve your goals.

3. Create a timeline for getting it done.

For example, perhaps one of your goals is to buy your first house after college within five years. That's a great goal. What are all of the things you need to do to achieve this? Some of your actions would include:

➡ Learn about loans and interest rates (buy books and/or attend a seminar).

➡ Establish a price range.

➡ Find out how much you need for a down payment and how long it will take you to save for it.

➡ Save, save, save.

➡ Meanwhile, learn about and compare the various neighborhoods and their resale potentials.

- ➡ Once you have the down payment, research and select a lender, and get pre-approved for a loan.

- ➡ Begin your search.

- ➡ Make an offer.

- ➡ Move in and live your dream.

Once you have listed all of the tasks you need to do, assign an approximate due date for each. Due dates keep you on task. Before you know it, you'll have accomplished your goal. Do this with every goal or dream you have.

Best Advice on Saving

Here's the best two pieces of advice I can give you about saving:

- ➡ Live below your means.

- ➡ Always allocate a percentage of your income as savings before you do *anything* else.

I grew up living these principles. When I received my first allowance at five years old my father told me, "I will give you this amount every Saturday at 9:00 a.m. *if* you do all of your chores during the week. Do not spend all of it right away. Put some of it into a box or jar and save it for something you really, really want or for an emergency." At five, I wasn't quite sure what kind of emergency I might have but I learned from the start not to spend 100 percent of any amount I received, even if it was one dollar.

Have the discipline to save *before* you spend. This can be very difficult if you are living paycheck to paycheck, but if you start monitoring your spending and lowering your expenses you will soon be saving, bit by bit.

> When trying to lose weight, you must eat less or exercise more. Similarly, when trying to save money you must spend less or make more.

Set up an automatic deposit into your savings account so that a portion of your paycheck is separate from your checking account. Then, pretend it's not there for a while. Out of sight, out of mind.

The amount I recommend saving is **15 percent** of your earnings. Start by saving up for six months of living expenses should you lose your job. Once you have that, start saving for your retirement, then for a wedding ring or marriage expenses, a honeymoon, a house, your child's education, vacations, a new car—whatever your goals include. Remember, a dollar saved is a dollar that has the potential to grow and each dollar that you keep helps you attain your goals sooner.

The key is to maximize your output at work and, in bad times, live with the minimum; in good times, save all of the excess and invest it.

Justifying Every Purchase

When I was in high school, peer pressure was fierce and I felt that I needed to have all of the latest and greatest material things to fit in with the other students. Fortunately, early on, my father taught me to justify my purchase of anything beyond the necessary costs of living. If I did not have a good rationalization, my father didn't hesitate to point it out. This taught me to think twice before buying something on impulse.

> "The safest way to double your money is to fold it over once and put it in your pocket."
>
> - Kin Hubbard, Humorist

Before pulling out *your* wallet always stop and ask yourself this one question:

Can I survive without it?

Have a plan for everything you do. Rewards come after periods of harvesting. As the old expression goes, we reap what we sow.

Monitoring Your Progress

Once you've established your financial plan and budget, you must, of course, stick to it or it won't happen. To make sure you do you must track the inflow and outflow of your money. Your plan and budget must always be at the forefront of your mind.

> Using software or an online tool is so much easier and faster than tracking your money manually. See chapter 12 for a list of tools.

Before taking cash out of the ATM, think about whether there's a less expensive alternative. Before making an impulse buy, think about whether you'd spend that money if your salary were reduced. Always justify the expense. Ask yourself if whatever it is you want to buy contributes to your wealth and well-being or if you're really just singing the it's-all-about-me song, "I want what I want when I want it and no one can stop me."

And you'd be right—the only person who can stop you...is you.

You, Your Family and Planning & Saving

Now I'm going to ask you a few questions about planning and saving.

➡ Has your family planned for its future? If so, how?

➡ How will you make sure your goals are accomplished?

7

Investing
Your Money

Dolphins can be found worldwide and are among the most intelligent animals. In fact, dolphins have two brains. Dolphin mothers care for their young closely and carefully. A baby dolphin spends the first several years of its life very near its mother watching and learning everything—from social skills, to hunting, to swimming. The mother carries its calf in its "slip stream," which is a hydrodynamic wake that develops as the mother swims, enabling her and her calf to stay up with their "pod" (their extended family, essentially).

Dolphins teach their young to ensure their survival and enhance their quality of life. Similarly, you want to learn about investing and growing your money to enhance your and your family's quality of life.

Meet the Grahams

Michael and Wendy Graham could write a manual on how to raise children and push them to their highest level. They set behavioral and performance standards sky high. They made sure their two children, Christine and Andrew, received an A-rated education but they did not pay for their children's college fees fully. Michael and Wendy wanted their kids to learn to work, earn, save, and appreciate money. Christine and Andrew also paid for their first cars. Most importantly, they learned from their parents how to invest a portion of what they earned wisely. Today, Christine and Andrew are successful financially as well as personally, professionally, and socially.

Meet the DeWitts

Patty and James DeWitt also have two children, Danny and Karen. Patty was extremely protective of her children and, as a result, Danny and Karen grew up dependent and not knowing how to do many things on their own—including earning and saving money—until they graduated from college and moved out.

At that point, they had to learn the hard way as many of us do. They lost money and time making expensive mistakes. It took a while but eventually they adapted in order to survive. They each took classes at the local community college on money management and investing. They are now, like Christine and Andrew Graham, very successful.

Why Invest?

Why invest? For two of the most important words you'll ever hear:

Compound Interest

First, let's talk about interest. **Interest** is the money that either you pay to use someone else's money or someone else pays you to use your money.

Let's say you loan a friend $1,000 (called the **principal** amount) so he or she can start a business. You both agree that your friend will pay you an annual 20 percent interest rate on the balance until it's paid off. Now, let's say your friend doesn't pay you anything at all for five years. You would add 20 percent to the balance each year, as follows:

Year	Balance	+ 20 %	Total
1	$1,000	$200	$1,200
2	$1,200	$240	$1,440
3	$1,440	$288	$1,728
4	$1,728	$346	$2,074
5	$2,074	$415	$2,488

At the end of five years, your friend would owe you $1,488 plus the original $1,000 you loaned him or her *without doing anything*. This additional money is called a **return on investment** (ROI). Good deal, right? For you, yes. Not so much for your friend, but that's the price you must pay for borrowing.

So, each year, the money added to the original principal amount also earns interest. This is called **compounding**. Compound interest, again, is the reason you *must* invest. Investment companies will pay you compound interest on the money you loan them or pay you dividends for investing in them.

Now, let's compare what happens to the same amount of money you have placed on a credit card (debt) versus investing it. Take a look at the following table.

	Credit Card	Investment
Balance/Amount	$10,000	$10,000
Interest	16% (owed)	8% (earned)
Monthly payment	$168	$155
In 10 years, you will have...	**Paid** **$20,102**	**Earned** **$19,120**

Time, in this case, is truly money. Have I convinced you yet? No? Then how about this...

If you begin putting $100 per month, starting at age 20, in an investment averaging eight percent interest your $100 will grow to be $95,950 by the time you're 45. But if you wait to start investing until you're 35, that same $100 will be only $20,000 by the time you're 45.

Put another way, with a three percent inflation rate, one dollar decreases in purchasing power to 64 cents over 15 years So if you place your money under a mattress each month instead, your $15,000 ($100 X 15 years) will decrease in purchasing power to $9,628 (64 cents X 15,000). What a bummer.

I think you now see why you must invest as early

> "The dutch paid 60 Guilder—$42.38 in U.S. dollars—to buy Manhattan in 1626. If that amount had been invested and compounded, it would be equal to $5.8 billion today."
>
> —Neale S. Godfrey

as possible. Compound interest is, quite simply, magic.

But...

There are risks in loaning your money out. Your friend's business could fail, he or she might go bankrupt, and you'd never get your original loan back—let alone any compound interest. Likewise, an investment company could make a bad investment and you could lose all or some of your original investment.

That's why you must **diversify**—spread out—your investments (called your portfolio), so that if one fails you don't lose everything. In other words, you don't want to put all of your eggs (money) in one basket (investment).

Diversification is the key to portfolio success. Selecting different investments, also called assets, enables you to maximize your returns while minimizing your risk. Investing is not about just stocks and bonds; it also includes businesses, real estate, and education.

So, how do you know what to invest in and what to shy away from? You can either spend years researching and studying this or you can find a Certified Financial Planner™ or wealth advisor you like and can trust, and who has a proven track record. You can find one at http://www.fpanet.org.

Learn the Lingo

If you choose to go the financial advisor route you should still take a basic investment course, read a good book on investing, or go online so that you:

➡ Learn the investment world lingo.

➡ Can talk about your investments knowledgeably with your advisor.

➡ Review and understand your portfolio statements.

For example, you may need to learn about terms such as gross domestic product (GDP), corporate earnings, liquidity, asset marketability, bull market, bear market, and dividends. Why? The behavior of these various elements will affect the performance of your money.

You should also become familiar with the types of market indexes including the Dow Jones Industrial Average, the S&P 500, the NASDAQ, the Wilshire 5000, and the Russell 3000.

Check out the investing glossary www.investmentword s.com.

Types of Investments

In addition to the lingo, you should learn about the types of investment you can make—again, to be able to make informed decisions.

Investments come in all shapes and sizes and differ in their level of risk, expected returns, and the length of time required to mature and pay you dividends. The basic investment choices include stocks, mutual funds (a group of stocks, bonds, and commodities), real estate, certificates of deposit (CDs), and bonds.

Investments & the Tax Man

When investing, taxes are an important consideration in choosing an investment account type. For example, if you invest in a 401(k) retirement account, you will be contributing money before taxes are taken out of your paycheck. You will, however, have to pay taxes when you cash it out at your retirement, but because of compound interest your final cash-out amount will be much higher than if you invested in an "after tax" account type.

If you work for a company that offers a retirement plan that matches some or all of the dollars you contribute, take advantage of it. This is the closest you'll come to free money.

Another type of account you should consider to minimize taxes is an IRA. Your contributions may be deductible depending on your adjusted gross income and your earnings.

Again, ask your financial advisor for advice. He or she will tailor your portfolio to your particular situation.

Investing in You

Finally, similar to diversifying your financial assets, to be successful over your lifetime, you must also diversify:

➡ Your intellectual assets (education, knowledge, and skills).

➡ Your social assets (networking, volunteering, mentoring).

➡ Your spiritual assets (growth and change).

Your Family & Investing

Once again, it's your turn. Think about your family and investing and answer the following questions.

➡ How did your grandparents earn and invest their money?

➡ How do your parents earn and invest their money?

➡ What are you doing to reinforce your skills and values related to earning and investing?

➡ How do you intend to break away from or be a model of your family's financial legacy?

8

Sharing & Protecting Your Money

The definition of **altruism** is giving without regard to reward or recognition. This selfless behavior was thought, until recently, to be a characteristic unique to humans. A study, however, showed that chimpanzees will help strangers—at personal cost, without expecting a reward. In experiments, chimps watched a person they had never seen before try to reach a wooden  stick that was within the chimp's reach. The chimps often brought the stick to the human—even if they had to climb eight feet out of their way to get it.

Male chimpanzees are also very protective of their communities, regularly patrolling their boundaries in search of intruders. In addition, they also share food with others in their group.

Like chimpanzees, we must contribute to and help our communities when and if we can, and we must protect our money to help future generations.

Juan Herrera

Juan Herrera, a well-educated business owner in his 40's, started his company right out of college and built it into a successful venture. He is now a multimillionaire. He was married in his late 20s but the relationship lasted only a few years. He never had children.

When I asked whether he had a will he said, "No. Why bother? I have no one to leave my money to. Quite honestly, I intend to keep every dollar I earned. I worked hard for it. Why should someone else benefit from the sweat off of *my* brow?"

Simon Cole

Simon Cole, also in his 40's, comes from a very humble background. Orphaned at a very early age, he was adopted at 12 and given an excellent education. Mr. Cole is now an extremely successful and wealthy businessperson, well known in his community. Mr. Cole is extremely grateful for what life has given him. He recently formed a foundation that helps children. He says, "Giving back is the most important thing I've done in my life."

He also wants to make sure his family and charities are provided for upon his death. Working with an attorney that specializes in estate planning, Mr. Cole's considerable assets now are protected and will be distributed upon his death to his family and foundation.

Philanthropy

Philanthropy is the act of donating money, goods, time, or effort to support a charitable cause—usually over an extended period with a defined objective. It includes any activity that promotes good or improves human quality of life.

Here's what author, comedian, and entertainer Steve Harvey says about philanthropy: "One simple thing my mother and father raised me with is the belief that you are blessed to become a blessing. It's paramount that we reach back and show others the road to success. If you know how to be successful, then it's vital that you share and teach others how to become successful."

Mr. Harvey began his philanthropy in 2000 by helping young people pursue their careers and educational dreams.

> "I have found that among its other benefits, giving liberates the soul of the giver."
>
> - Maya Angelou

Recently, he founded the Steve Harvey Foundation (www.steveharveyfoundation.com), whose mission is to:

➡ Improve public schools in urban areas by upgrading facilities and purchasing books, technology, and other essential resources.

➡ Provide educational and mentoring opportunities for middle and high school students so that they can envision and realize their dreams.

Another famous philanthropist is Bill Gates, who founded Microsoft Corporation in 1975. Mr. Gates is one of the wealthiest people in the world. He and his wife established the Bill and Melinda Gates Foundation (www.gatesfoundation.org) in 2000. Its mission is to enhance healthcare and reduce extreme poverty all over the world, and to expand educational opportunities and access to information technology in the United States. The interests and passions of the Gates family has driven the foundation to be the largest in the world.

Actress Angelina Jolie donates one third of her income to charity. She travels extensively as the United Nations' High Commissioner for Refugees. She and Brad Pitt started the Jolie-Pitt Foundation in 2006 to assist with humanitarian crises around the world.

> "Remember that the happiest people are not those getting more, but those giving more."
>
> - H. Jackson Brown, Author

Other famous philanthropists include Oprah Winfrey, Bono, J.K. Rowling, and Warren Buffett.

Why Do We Give?

Giving our time, energy, and money contributes to our need to find meaning in life and to feel connected to our communities. It also gives us internal satisfaction and purpose.

My dad always said to me, "Help by teaching others how to obtain success." That philosophy helped me choose my profession. As a financial planner, I teach people how to save, manage, invest, share, and protect their money with the goal of being financially independent.

In speaking with people about philanthropy and altruism I find common themes. It makes people feel revitalized and truly happy to help others. "It brings us together as a community," one person told me. "It's the right thing to do," another wealthy client of mine said.

"No one ever became poor by giving."

- Anne Frank

Charities

Charity is the practice of generous giving. A charity is also an institution, organization, or fund whose purpose is to help the needy or support a cause.

There are thousands of charities and foundations—many address specific issues or problems as shown here.

Cause	Sample Organizations

Children	The Children's Initiative
	Educate Tomorrow
	Believe in Tomorrow
	CIMA
Health/Medical	Susan G. Komen Breast Cancer Foundation
	American Red Cross
	World Health and Education Foundation
Underprivileged	Habitat for Humanity
	United Way
	National Coalition for the Homeless
Environmental	World Wildlife Fund
	Wildlife Conservation Society
	The Rainforest Foundation
Disabilities	Special Olympics
	National Mental Health Association
	The American Veterans Disabled for Life Memorial
Hunger	ChildFund International
	Feed the Hunger Foundation
	Help End Hunger Now Foundation

All of these organizations have websites (see chapter 12), and most allow you to donate online.

There are several ways to make charitable contributions. You can:

➡ Give an outright gift.

➡ Make a bequest in your will.

➡ Set up a charitable trust or foundation.

There are also Web sites that enable you to shop and give. Two of them are www.Igive.com and www.justgive.org. On Igive.com, you select a favorite cause—or add a new one—and then shop at over 700 name brand online stores. A portion of each of your purchases is donated to your selected cause. And, products don't cost more than anywhere else.

> Anything you donate to charity may qualify as a tax deduction.

JustGive.org allows you to purchase charity gift cards you can give as gifts to family and friends, which they can redeem to support their favorite causes.

What Would You Do With $1 Million?

Imagine that someone gave you one million dollars and said, "You can't keep it. You must invest in a charitable cause."

➡ Which organizations would you choose and why?

➡ How will your project enhance the quality of people's lives?

➡ Why is it important to you and the world?

Giving Your Time When You Don't Have Money

A young client of mine said to me recently, "I'm not rich so I can't give a lot of money, but I give my time. Volunteering, for me, is a win-win. Others get help and I get to feel good about myself."

A friend said to me the other day, "I just dropped off a carload full of toys and clothes

> "It is one of the most beautiful compensations in this life that no man can sincerely try to help another without helping himself."
>
> - Ralph Waldo Emerson

my kids don't use any more at the women and children's center. The women were so grateful, the children were delighted, and I felt amazing."

If you don't have money to share, you can share yourself—your talents, your brains, your skills—with others who need a helping hand. Here are some ideas that cost very little or nothing.

➡ Volunteer your time to a charitable organization.

➡ Donate old or new belongings.

➡ Host a party for the benefit of an organization.

➡ Give the money in your coin jar to your favorite charity.

Planning for a Potential Crisis

I don't have a crystal ball that enables me to see into the future, unfortunately—and neither do you. So you must protect yourself and your assets. Make sure you protect:

➡ Your salary, in case of disability (you are more likely to become disabled than to die prematurely).

➡ Your home, in case of fire, hurricane, tornado, earthquake, or flood.

➡ Your car, in case of an accident.

➡ Your relatives who depend on your earnings, by having life insurance.

➡ The assets you accumulate before you marry, by having a pre-nuptial (property settlement) agreement.

You also need to make sure you have the proper documents to take care of your family in case you die suddenly. If you are a parent, your will needs to name the individual who will take care of your children if you or your spouse can't for any reason.

I know it's hard for people, especially when young, to think about these things, but it's the responsible and right thing to do. Think about who will be impacted after you die.

Legal documents such as powers of attorney, wills, and trusts can save your **beneficiaries** (the people who will receive your assets), time, money, and some grief.

Estate Planning

Estate planning is the process of arranging for the disposal or distribution of all of your assets, including money and property. As you get older and begin to accumulate wealth it's important for you to plan your estate with an estate-planning attorney. In general, you can pass your assets on to your beneficiaries through:

- Contracts (such as life insurance policies, IRA, 401(k) plans).

- Titles (such as home or automobile).

- Wills or living trusts.

Durable Power of Attorney

Your parents are legally permitted to make decisions for you until the age of 18. However, once you turn 18, you have the right to make your own choice as to who has your power of attorney.

A **durable power of attorney** is a document drafted by an attorney that lets someone you choose act on your behalf if you are injured or incapable (for example, if you were to be in an accident or develop a medical condition that incapacitated you). Typically, these types of decisions involve financial or medical decisions.

Financial decisions include how to pay your bills and distribution of cash and assets. Medical decisions include a do-not-resuscitate order or "yes" or "no" on tube feeding.

If you don't name anyone to take charge, your property or assets can be lost or stolen. The best person to give this authority to is someone you trust, who is emotionally and financially stable, who has the power to be objective, and who has your best interests in mind. Think about whether it would be your parent, another relative, a best friend, or your spouse. This person will most likely change over time as you age.

Wills

Your **will** is a legal document that dictates how your assets will be distributed after your death. Typically, you need a will once you marry or have children.

Your will also names an **executor**, that is, the person who will see that your wishes are carried out. Legally, this defaults to your closest blood relative if you have not named someone in your will, but that person may not be capable of or want to be your executor. And if they don't, the court system becomes your executor.

> Fifty-eight percent of Americans do not have a will.

Too many people don't create wills and end up leaving decisions to the court system. Courts are typically underfunded and backlogged, so the distribution of your assets can take a long, long time. Why put your beneficiaries through that? They are sad enough that you died.

All wills must go through the **probate** process, which is the legal process of administering the estate of a deceased person ensuring his or her instructions are followed and creditors are paid.

Living Trusts

Living trusts don't replace wills. In fact, they are sometimes included with wills and power of attorney documents. As opposed to a will, a living trust takes effect while you are alive. You create it to "hold" assets during and after your life.

Trusts are recommended for assets that need to be out of your estate for tax and distribution purposes. There are several types of trusts, and you should hire an attorney who specializes in trusts to help you decide which is best for you.

Communicating Your Wishes to Your Family

It's vital that you communicate to your family how and why you made the estate plan decisions you did and how you wish for them to be executed. Why? After you're gone, certain family members may not understand your decision-making process. It happens too often and can ruin relationships and destroy families. Why? Because money can often bring out the worst in people. Sadly, greed often rears its ugly head in spades during a time when families need to support one another.

For example, a man left 15 percent of his estate to one child and 85 percent to another—with no explanation. The one who was left the smaller portion took her sibling to court. They now hate one another and refuse to be in the same house, let alone room, at family gatherings.

In another case, a mother told one of her daughters that she wanted her to have her engagement ring but the mother neglected to say this in her will. Her son, who was the will's executor, sold the ring when the mother died, intending to split the money with his other siblings, along with the rest of the estate proceeds. The daughter who was promised the ring sued her brother. The lesson? If you want to give a particular item to someone, make sure it's in your will.

Keep It Current

It's also important to keep your will or trust updated because things change over time. You may have named a parent or uncle as your executor but since then he or she died.

Protecting Your Other Assets

It's also important to talk about protecting your other assets. Protecting your intellectual assets is mostly about nurturing your brain and being smart about your habits and health. Exercise your mind with books, workshops, and classes. Never stop learning. Learn something new every day. Nurture your body as well. You are what you eat and drink.

In terms of protecting your social assets, you must be careful with your reputation. Reputation takes a long time to build but just seconds to lose. Always "do unto others as you want them to do unto you." Try to put yourself in the other person's position to see their viewpoint.

Preserve and grow your spiritual assets by seeking to always evolve and learn from your mistakes. Every challenge is an opportunity to learn. Always look at the bright side. Stay away from negativity if you can, but if you encounter it, try to channel it into positive energy.

How Does Your Family Protect & Share Money

Think about how your family has protected their money and answer the following questions.

➡ Is your family protecting itself for the future? If so, how?

➡ How does your family feel about giving to and helping others in need?

➡ What are you doing (or plan to do) to improve our world?

9

Putting It All Together

I'm going to tell you one last story. This is a tale of two people, Raymond and Theresa, who did everything I just described in this book over the last 30 years, and what the results of their decisions meant for them and how they impacted their world.

Raymond grew up the sixth of six children. Only his dad had a high school diploma; his mom had to leave school early to earn money. Raymond's dad served in World War II and the Korean War. While he was gone, his wife worked full time to support their children. In between and after the wars, Raymond's dad held numerous jobs. Money was tight, but they always managed to scrape by.

Raymond also worked from the time he was 12 to help his family out. He mowed lawns, shoveled snow, and worked in a grocery store. The worst job he had was when he was 17. He was assigned to clean out gelatin from oven vents at a large manufacturing plant. It was the grossest thing he'd ever done. But money is money and he did what he had to do to survive.

Raymond graduated from high school and went to college, but dropped out after too much partying caused him to fail his courses. Raymond went to work in a warehouse but, after a year, realized that he had more to offer the world than driving a forklift around all day.

He enrolled in college again and graduated with a technical degree. After graduation, Raymond found a job as a programmer at a high-tech company.

Theresa grew up in a middle class family. Her dad emigrated from Italy when he was in his early 20's. He started and ran a small Italian restaurant all of his life. He met and married Theresa's mom, a factory worker, a few years after emigrating. Theresa is the third of six children.

From the time she was 12, Theresa worked. She babysat, she waitressed in her father's restaurant, and she worked as a stock clerk in a drug store. After she graduated from high school, Theresa went to a local community college for two years to reduce her education and housing costs. In the summers, Theresa worked full time to earn money for her books and tuition. She also applied for and received a student loan. After finishing her degree, Theresa landed a job at the same high-tech company Raymond worked for.

Theresa and Raymond met on Theresa's first day at work. Shortly thereafter, they fell in love and got married.

The company Theresa and Raymond worked for gave them small amounts of stock as part of their compensation. Not knowing anything about stock, they shrugged because they didn't think it would affect them much. They both made sure they were contributing the maximum allowed to their 401(k) retirement plans.

As luck would have it, the personal computer market was just taking off and their company began to make enormous profits. They began to receive larger and larger quarterly employee bonuses. They stashed every cent of the bonuses in the bank. Houses were expensive where they lived and they were going to need a very large down payment.

A few years later, Theresa decided she wanted to do freelance work and left the company to start her own business. She earned triple what she earned the year before. They banked most of that, too. She also packed as much as she could into a SEP IRA retirement account.

Other than contributing to retirement accounts, Raymond and Theresa knew next to nothing about investing. They had heard they should but didn't know how to go about it. One day, they saw a flyer for a financial planning class at the local community college. Taking that class changed their lives.

On the first day, Theresa and Raymond walked into the classroom, sat down, and looked around the room. They noticed they were the youngest people there—by at least 20 years.

The teacher introduced himself and said he was a financial planner. He went around the room and asked everyone what their goals were for the class. Theresa and Raymond said that they wanted to learn how to invest their money and make more. A man in his mid 40's said, "I need to save for my kid's education." When the teacher asked him how old his kids were, the man said, "14 and 16." The teacher was frank and said, "You've started too late. You have a lot of catching up to do." Another couple in their 50's were concerned about whether they'd been saving enough for retirement.

After the class was over, Raymond and Theresa hired the teacher to help them invest their savings.

Meanwhile, Theresa's business grew and, within five years, she had 50 people employees on her payroll. During this time, Theresa and Raymond also bought a house and had two children, a boy and girl, who they raised to value hard work and the power of money.

Meanwhile, Raymond's company became a Fortune 50 company. His stocks grew rapidly and, soon, they were sitting on a small fortune. They sold their house and bought a bigger house. They bought a second vacation property on a lake. They spent time and money fixing up both houses. They sold their vacation house for a very large profit several years later and bought another one in the mountains.

At 46, Raymond decided to leave the technology business and do something else that would give back to society. He wanted to help educate children because he knew that education is the foundation of success. He went back to school, earned his teaching credential, and got a job as a math teacher at an urban high school in a lower income area of the city.

A year later, Theresa sold her business. She and Raymond also sold their home for another enormous profit and bought, fixed up, and flipped two more right before the housing market began to crash.

Theresa became a consultant to small business owners, helping them to build and grow their companies.

Theresa and Raymond's children are now in college and on their way to becoming independent, productive members of society. They work part-time while going to school and full-time in the summers.

Theresa and Raymond own their homes and two cars outright. They have more than enough savings in their retirement account to see them through the later stages of their lives. They have a trust that provides for their family and two selected charities.

So, here's the thing, if Theresa and Raymond can do it, anyone can. *You* can.

10

Sharing Your Discoveries

One of the best gifts you can give to your family—and one that costs nothing—is to teach them about personal finance. This will prove to be a far greater legacy than any inheritance you might one day leave behind. Involve your parents, your siblings, and the rest of your family in your discoveries.

One of the Primary sources of financial literacy is through family members.

In many families, parents give up their own goals to give their children a better life and, in the process, they sacrifice their own education, limiting their ability to teach their children certain life skills—such as financial literacy—they need to be successful. And, so, the cycle never ends.

So teach them everything you learn. It's never too late for anyone. Model good financial behavior to serve as an incentive for other family members, including any children you may have.

I recommend:

➡ Having family financial learning meetings.

➡ Pooling your money, investing it together, and watching it grow.

➡ Agreeing on a good cause and working on it together.

➡ Finding ways to be connected (such as using Google, Yahoo, or Facebook group).

Life is about family and money. They both matter for you to be the most successful person possible.

Good luck to you and I wish you continued happiness and success.

I would love it if you shared your money and life lessons with me. You can reach me at contact@elainekingcfp.com.

Why Not Use social networks to communicate your savings goals?

–Farnoosh Torabi

11

Resources

This chapter contains a list of books about family, wealth, and money management should you want more information. I've also included a list of websites that you can use as additional resources.

Recommended Books

➡ *Family Wealth—Keeping It in the Family: How Family Members and Their Advisers Preserve Human, Intellectual, and Financial Assets for Generations*, James E. Hughes Jr., Bloomberg Press, 2004.

➡ *Wealth in Families*, Charles W. Collier, Harvard University, 2006.

➡ *The Legacy Family: The Definitive Guide to Creating a Successful Multigenerational Family*,

Lee Hausner and Douglas K. Freeman, Palgrave Macmillan, 2009.

➡ *The Wall Street Journal Complete Personal Finance Guidebook*, Jeff D. Opdyke, Three Rivers Press, 2006.

➡ *The Motley Fool Investment Guide for Teens: 8 Steps to Having More Money Than Your Parents Ever Dreamed Of*, Tom Gardner, David Gardner, and Selena Maranjian, Fireside, 2002.

➡ *The Ultimate Gift*, Jim Stovall, Executive Books, 2000.

➡ *Money Doesn't Grow On Trees: A Parent's Guide to Raising Financially Responsible Children*, Neale S. Godfrey and Carolina Edwards, Fireside, 2006.

➡ *Every Day is a Gift*, Barry Gottlieb, Simple Truths, 2010.

➡ *One Family's Story—A Primer on Bowen Theory*, Michael E. Kerr, MD, Bowen Center for the Study of the Family, 2005.

Recommended Websites

➡ Free money management utility (www.mint.com)

➡ Free saving "piggy bank" site (www.smartypig.com)

➡ Secret Millionaires Club for kids site (www.smckids.com)

➡ Charity gift card site (www.justgive.org)

- ➡ Shop and give to your favorite cause (www.igive.com)

- ➡ Money advice, tools, and calculators (www.lifetuner.org)

- ➡ Quicken money management software (www.quicken.intuit.com)

- ➡ Investment term dictionary (www.investorwords.com)

- ➡ Business term dictionary (www.businessdictionary.com)

- ➡ Credit report information (www.creditreport.com)

- ➡ Financial Planning Association (www.fpanet.org)

- ➡ Digital storytelling (www.memoirproduction.com)

- ➡ Steve Harvey Foundation (www.steveharveyfoundation.com)

- ➡ Bill and Melinda Gates Foundation (www.gatesfoundation.org)

- ➡ The Children's Initiative (www.childrensinitiative.org)

- ➡ Educate Tomorrow (www.educatetomorrow.org)

- ➡ Believe in Tomorrow (www.believeintomorrow.org)

- ➡ CIMA (www.cimahope.org)

- Susan G. Komen Breast Cancer Foundation (www.komen.org)

- American Red Cross (www.redcross.org)

- World Health and Education Foundation (www.worldhealth-ed.org)

- Habitat for Humanity (www.habitat.org)

- United Way (www.liveunited.org)

- National Coalition for the Homeless (www.nationalhomeless.org)

- World Wildlife Fund (www.worldwildlife.org)

- Wildlife Conservation Society (www.wcs.org)

- The Rainforest Foundation (www.rainforestfoundation.org)

- Special Olympics (www.specialolympics.org)

- National Mental Health Association (www.nmha.org)

- The American Veterans Disabled for Life Memorial (www.avdlm.org)

- ChildFund International (www.childfund.org)

- Feed the Hunger Foundation (www.feed-hunger.com)

- Help End Hunger Now Foundation (www.helpendhungernow.org)

Terms Used in this Book

Appreciation
The increase in value of an asset.

Asset
Something valuable that you own, benefit from, or have use of.

Bankruptcy
A legal declaration that you are unable to pay your debts.

Beneficiaries
People who will receive your assets when you die.

Bequest
Something left to somebody in a will.

Budget
A plan that distributes future personal income towards expenses, savings, and debt repayment.

Capital

Cash or goods used to produce income by investing in either a business or income property.

Credit

A contractual agreement in which you receive something of value now and agree to repay the lender at some later date.

Charity

The practice of generous giving; an institution, organization, or fund whose purpose is to help the needy or support a cause.

Checking Account

A bank account that enables you to make withdrawals or payments to other people using checks or a debit card.

Commodity

An item that is bought and sold.

Compound interest

Interest that is calculated not only on the initial principal but also on the accumulated interest of prior periods.

Credit card

A plastic card issued by a bank that allows you to purchase goods and services and pay for them later, often with interest.

Credit rating

An estimate of the amount of credit that can be extended to a company or person without undue risk.

Credit Report

A summary of your financial history.

Debit card

A plastic card issued by a bank that you can use to pay for purchases; the money is transferred directly from the your checking account to the seller's business bank account.

Debt

An amount owed to a person or an organization for money borrowed.

Delayed gratification

The ability to wait in order to get something that you want; also called impulse control, will power, and self-control.

Depreciation

The decrease in value of an asset.

Diversification

A portfolio strategy designed to reduce exposure to risk by combining a variety of investments, such as stocks, bonds, and real estate.

Dividends

Company profits paid to stockholders, either in cash or in more shares of stock.

Drive

An internal force that powers you forward to success and helps you achieve your dreams.

Durable Power of Attorney

A document drafted by an attorney that lets someone you choose act on your behalf if you are injured or become incapable.

Estate planning

The process of arranging for the disposal or distribution of all of your assets, including money and property.

Executor

The person who will see that your will is carried out.

Expense

The amount of money spent to buy or do something.

Finances

The science of the management of money and other assets.

Financial literacy

The ability to make knowledgeable and successful decisions about using and managing your money.

Fixed Expense

A cost that does not change from period to period or that changes only very slightly.

Fortune 500

The top 500 companies in the United States as listed by *Fortune* magazine.

Income

Money received over a period of time either as payment for work, goods, or services, or as profit on capital.

Interest

The fee charged by a lender for the use of borrowed money, usually expressed as an annual percentage of the principal.

Investment

The purchase of a financial product or other item of value with an expectation that it will grow in value and make you more money.

Liability

A legal obligation to pay a debt.

Living trust

A written legal document which could substitute for a will as your primary estate planning vehicle.

Loan

An amount of money given to somebody on the condition that it will be paid back later.

Money

A method of exchange issued by a government in the form of coins of gold, silver or other metal, or paper bills that is used as the measure of the value of goods and services.

Mortgage

A loan to finance the purchase of real estate, usually with specified payment periods and interest rates.

net worth

Your assets minus your liabilities.

Passion

A strong liking or enthusiasm for a subject or activity.

Philanthropy

The act of donating money, goods, time, or effort to support a charitable cause—usually over an extended period with a defined objective.

Portfolio

A collection of investments.

Power of Attorney

See *Durable Power of Attorney*.

Principal

The amount borrowed.

Probate

The legal process of administering the estate of a deceased person that ensures his or her instructions are followed and creditors are paid.

Return on investment (ROI)

A calculation used to determine whether an investment is wise and how well it will repay you.

Savings Account

A deposit account at a bank or savings and loan that pays interest, but cannot be withdrawn by check writing.

Stock

A share of the ownership of a company.

Success

The achievement of something planned or attempted; the attainment of fame, wealth, or power; something that turns out as planned or intended.

Transaction

An agreement between a buyer and a seller to exchange an asset for payment.

Variable Expense

A cost that changes significantly from period to period.

Will

A legal document, valid when you die, that dictates how your assets will be distributed.

About the Author

Elaine King provides families with financial planning strategies and helping them understand, organize, and manage their wealth. She also advises her clients on retirement planning, saving for education, estate planning, and financial competency (for both parents and children).

Elaine grew up in Peru and has lived, worked, and studied in Austria, Canada, Japan, Mexico, and the United States. She received an MBA degree from Thunderbird, the American School of International Management. She also completed a postgraduate program at the Bowen Center for the Study of Family.

Elaine is a Florida Supreme Court Certified Family Mediator, a Certified Financial Planner® professional, and a Certified Divorce Financial Analyst.™ She has also served as the President of the Financial Planning Association of Miami-Dade (2010-2011).

Elaine has appeared on CBS and Univision, and has been quoted by the *Wall Street Journal,* the *Journal of Financial Planning, The Miami Herald, Time* magazine, *Business Week, Financial Planning Magazine*, and other national news publications.

Elaine also mentors children for Educate Tomorrow and supports CIMA, a shelter for homeless children in her native Peru.

To reach Elaine, e-mail her at **contact@elainekingcfp.com**.

Made in the USA
Las Vegas, NV
09 March 2022

45301250R00066